THE ROCK WE EAT:
SALT

Library of Congress Cataloging-in-Publication Data

Strom, Laura Layton.
    The rock we eat : salt / by Laura Layton Strom.
        p. cm. -- (Shockwave)
    Includes index.
    ISBN-10: 0-531-17799-8 (lib. bdg.)
    ISBN-13: 978-0-531-17799-0 (lib. bdg.)
    ISBN-10: 0-531-15487-4 (pbk.)
    ISBN-13: 978-0-531-15487-8 (pbk.)
1. Salt--Juvenile literature. I. Title. II. Series.

    TN900.S9 2007
    664'.4--dc22

2007008939

Published in 2008 by Children's Press, an imprint of Scholastic Inc.,
557 Broadway, New York, New York 10012
www.scholastic.com

08 09 10 11 12 13 14 15 16 17
10 9 8 7 6 5 4 3 2 1

Printed in China through Colorcraft Ltd., Hong Kong

Author: Laura Layton Strom
Educational Consultant: Ian Morrison
Editor: Karen Alexander
Designer: Avon Willis
Photo Researcher: Jamshed Mistry
Illustration: Ellen Giggenbach

Photographs by: Aapimage.com: AP Photo/Douglas C. Pizac (JCB Dieselmax, p. 15);
EPA/Pierre Holtz (p. 30); **Avon Willis** (p. 5); **Big Stock Photo** (rock salt, pp. 22–23);
© **Erwin & Peggy Bauer/hedgehoghouse.com** (p. 14); © **Gemma Hayward/
photographersdirect.com** (p. 3); **Jennifer and Brian Lupton** (teenage girl, p. 33);
More Images/North Wind Picture Archives (Southern blockade runner, p. 17);
Photolibrary (pp. 7–9; Dead Sea swimmer, p. 15; p. 16; Mahatma Gandhi, p. 19;
p. 21; satellite photo of Zagros Mountains, p. 23; pp. 25–28; selling salt, p. 29;
child labor, pp. 32–33); **www.stockcentral.co.nz:** age fotostock (salt collecting, p. 29)
Topfoto (p. 10); **Tranz:** Corbis (cover; Maras salt terraces, p. 11; p. 13; Bonneville Salt
Flats, p. 15; planes underground, p. 17; p. 18; Indian people gathering salt, p. 19; p. 20;
underground salt mine, p. 22; salt dome in Yemen, p. 23; p. 24; p. 31); Rex Features
(Wieliczka Salt Mine statues, p. 11)

All illustrations and other photographs © Weldon Owen Education Inc.

SHOCKWAVE
SOCIAL STUDIES

THE ROCK WE EAT: SALT

LAURA LAYTON STROM

children's press®
An imprint of Scholastic Inc.
NEW YORK • TORONTO • LONDON • AUCKLAND • SYDNEY
MEXICO CITY • NEW DELHI • HONG KONG
DANBURY, CONNECTICUT

CHECK THESE OUT!

SHOCKER
Stuff to Shock, Surprise, and Amaze You

Quick Recaps and Notable Notes

Word Stunners and Other Oddities

The Heads-Up on Expert Reading

Links to More Information

CONTENTS

HIGH-POWERED WORDS   6

GET ON THE WAVELENGTH   8

Salty History   10

As Precious as Salt   12

Salty Customs   13

Salty Sites   14

Salt Wars   16

Harvesting Salt   20

   Seawater   20

   Salt Lakes   21

   Rock Salt   22

   Salt Domes   23

Simply Add Salt   24

Blood, Sweat, and Tears   26

The Salt Trade   28

Child Salt Workers   30

AFTERSHOCKS   32

GLOSSARY   34

FIND OUT MORE   35

INDEX   36

ABOUT THE AUTHOR   36

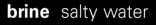
brine salty water

electrolyte (*i LEK truh lite*) a material that conducts electricity and that can be dissolved in liquid

evaporate (*ee VAP uh rate*) to change from a liquid into a vapor, or gas

mineral (*MIN ur uhl*) a natural matter that is not a plant or an animal

pickle to preserve vegetables, fruit, or meat in salt or vinegar

solar (*SOH lur*) to do with the sun

substance (*SUHB stuhnss*) a material that can be seen or weighed

· ·

For additional vocabulary, see Glossary on page 34.

In the word *electrolyte*, *electro* relates to electricity. The *-lyte* suffix, or ending, refers to a substance that can be broken down by a specific process.

Evaporation ponds
at La Palma, Spain

Early humans didn't add salt to their food. They got all the salt they needed from the meat they ate. However, gradually people realized how precious salt was. Salt preserved their food so they could keep it to eat later. It also added flavor to their food.

Salt was once thought to be very rare. People treasured it. They traded for salt. They built roads just to transport salt. They fought wars over salt. They even used salt for money.

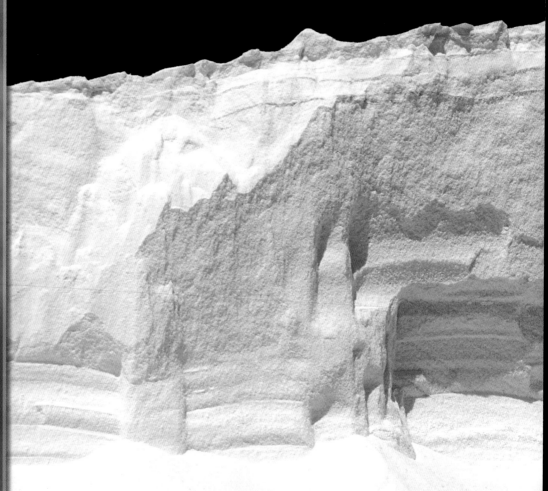

Salt mountain at Walvis Bay, Namibia, Africa

Now people know that there is salt in nearly every place in the world. However, salt mining and the salt trade are still important. Our bodies need salt to work properly. Salt has many uses in our daily lives. We may take salt for granted, but we cannot live without it.

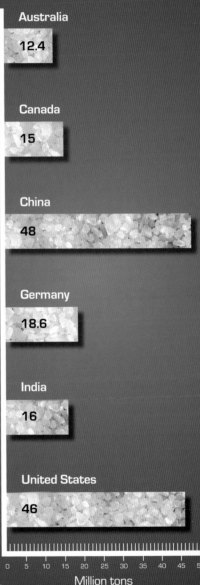

SALT PRODUCTION

The graph shows an estimate of how many millions of tons of salt the major salt-producing countries produced in 2006.

Australia

12.4

Canada

15

China

48

Germany

18.6

India

16

United States

46

0   5   10   15   20   25   30   35   40   45   50

Million tons

SALTY HISTORY

People in China began to gather salt crystals about 8,000 years ago. Then, about 2,500 years ago, they began to produce salt. They boiled **brine** in iron pans until the water **evaporated.** Only salt was left. Their method spread to Europe. For 2,000 years, that was the main way in which salt was produced.

A double gate that was once part of the Via Salaria

Salt was so important to the Romans that they built a road to transport it. The Via Salaria, or Salt Road, was about 145 miles long. It ran from one side of Italy to the other. The Greeks also prized salt. They believed that once you had eaten salt with a person, you were friends for life.

The salt mine at Wieliczka in Poland has been worked for more than 900 years. It is the biggest salt mine in the world. Its tunnels go down 1,000 feet. The mine has a museum and churches. It has large rooms where concerts can be held.

SALTY SAYING

The word salary comes from sal. Sal is the Latin word for salt. Roman soldiers were paid in salt. People who are "worth their salt" are worth their pay.

Statues made of salt, Wieliczka Salt Mine

The salt **terraces** at Maras in Peru were built more than 600 years ago. They are fed by a saltwater spring far up in the mountains. People still work the salt terraces today.

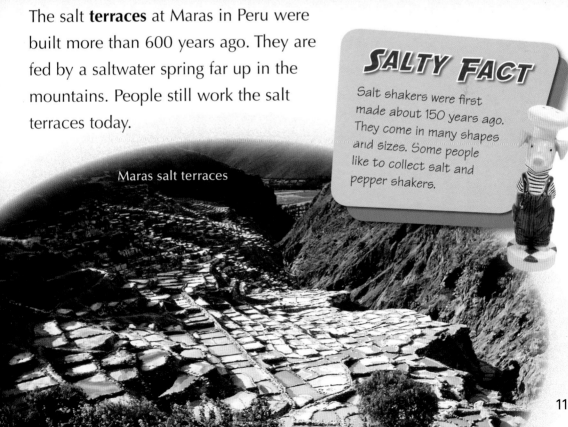

Maras salt terraces

As Precious as Salt

A FOLKTALE FROM EUROPE

Once, long ago, a king asked his daughter how much she loved him.

"You are as precious to me as salt," she replied.

The king was hurt by his daughter's answer.
He thought she was making fun of him.
He thought she didn't care about him.

Soon after, the king decided to have a great feast. His daughter told the cook to make every dish without salt. Nothing tasted good.

After the feast, the girl told her father what she had done. The king realized how important salt was. He also realized that his daughter did love him.

SALTY CUSTOMS

Some people think it is bad luck to spill salt. They throw some of the salt back over their left shoulder so the bad luck won't happen. There are many other customs about salt.

- In the Middle East, people often used salt to seal bargains.

- Some people think that you shouldn't offer salt to someone at the table. It will bring sadness to them.

- Some sailors believe it is bad luck to mention salt when they are at sea.

- In many countries, guests are welcomed with bread and salt. It is a sign of friendship.

- In France, babies often had salt put on them to protect them. In Holland, the salt was put in the baby's bed.

- In Japan, sumo wrestlers sprinkle salt before a fight. They believe this will prevent them from getting injured.

SALTY SAYING

Someone who is "the salt of the earth" is a good person. The saying may refer to the great value of salt.

Sumo wrestlers

SALTY SITES

Places near salt works often have in their name a word that means salt. The German word for salt is *salz*. Salzburg is a town in Austria. There are four salt mines near it. The salt mine at Hallstatt in Austria is one of the oldest in the world. *Hals* is a Greek word meaning salt. In England, place-names ending in *wich* are often found near salt works. Salt has been produced at Northwich in England since Roman times.

The word *lick* in an American place-name often means that animals went there to lick salt from the rocks, salt beds, or water. That is how Elk Lick in Pennsylvania and Lick in Ohio got their names. Some of the first trails in America were made by buffalo looking for salt.

SALTY NAMES

Have you heard of these "salty" U.S. place-names?

Salt Lake City, Utah

Salina, New York

Saline Valley, California

Salton Sea, California

Saltville, Virginia

Grand Saline, Texas

The word *saline* refers to anything with salt in it. A saline solution is water with salt in it.

Buffalo at a salt lick in Montana

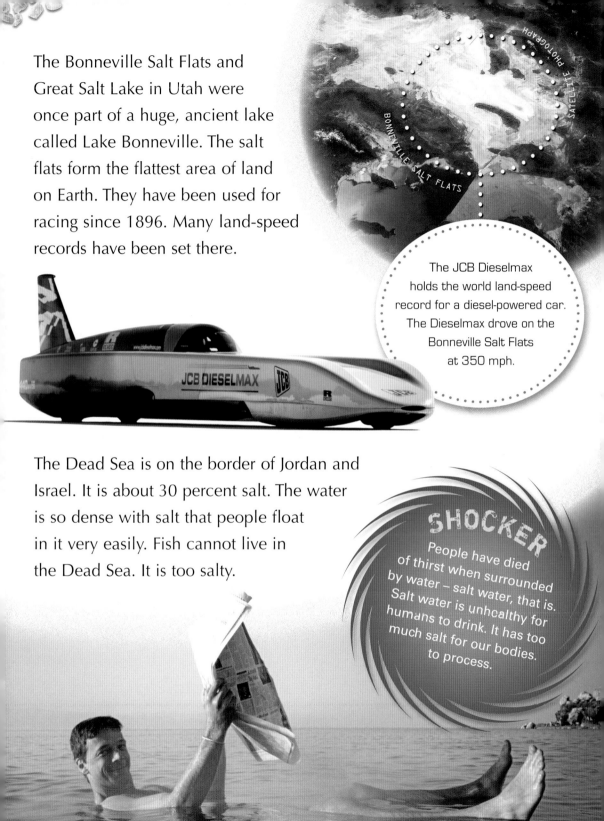

The Bonneville Salt Flats and Great Salt Lake in Utah were once part of a huge, ancient lake called Lake Bonneville. The salt flats form the flattest area of land on Earth. They have been used for racing since 1896. Many land-speed records have been set there.

BONNEVILLE SALT FLATS

The JCB Dieselmax holds the world land-speed record for a diesel-powered car. The Dieselmax drove on the Bonneville Salt Flats at 350 mph.

JCB DIESELMAX

The Dead Sea is on the border of Jordan and Israel. It is about 30 percent salt. The water is so dense with salt that people float in it very easily. Fish cannot live in the Dead Sea. It is too salty.

SHOCKER

People have died of thirst when surrounded by water – salt water, that is. Salt water is unhealthy for humans to drink. It has too much salt for our bodies to process.

Man floating in the Dead Sea

SALT WARS

For hundreds of years, whoever had control of the salt supplies had great power. People needed salt, so the owners of salt beds could charge high prices. They could also control people and countries by not letting them have access to salt unless they did as they were told.

- More than 2,000 years ago, Rome got money for wars by increasing the price of salt.

- In fourteenth-century Europe, anyone preparing for war began by salting meat and fish for the army's food supplies.

- In the eighteenth century, France put a tax on salt. Many people **smuggled** salt from places where it was cheaper. The French people were very angry about the tax. It was one of the reasons for the French **Revolution**.

People rioting at the beginning of the French Revolution

SHOCKER

Imagine dying from a small wound! That is what happened to many French soldiers in Napoleon's army in the early 1800s. There was not enough salt to clean their wounds.

During the American Revolution (1775–1783), the British cut off the settlers' salt supply. They **blockaded** American ports. They also destroyed many of the Atlantic saltworks. However, the settlers found other ways to get salt. They set up saltworks along the east coast. It was the beginning of the huge American salt industry.

Controlling salt gave people power:
- owners could charge high prices
- owners could deny access to salt
- owners could control whole armies with salt

Salt was also important in the American **Civil War** (1861–1865). The South imported most of its salt. The North blockaded southern ports. Northern soldiers destroyed any saltworks they found. The shortage of salt in the South was very bad. Newspapers told people how to make salt. They also printed articles on how to preserve food without using salt. One newspaper suggested that the best way to keep meat from going bad in summer was to eat it in spring!

A Southern blockade runner trying to avoid a Northern ship

The salt beds near El Paso, Texas

In 1877, a battle was fought over the salt beds near El Paso, Texas. El Paso had been part of Mexico. Under Mexican law, the salt beds were in common ownership. The salt could be gathered free by anyone. El Paso had become part of the United States in 1848. Under American law, people could apply for ownership of the salt beds.

Some American businessmen tried to get ownership of the salt beds. They wanted to charge people for the salt. The local people objected. The dispute resulted in the wounding or killing of several people. It nearly led to a war between the United States and Mexico.

?

I had trouble understanding what *common ownership* meant. But when I read the next sentence, it became much clearer. Reading on often helps with new or difficult words or expressions.

From the late 1700s until 1947, India was a British **colony**. Mahatma Gandhi was an Indian political and spiritual leader. He believed in nonviolent protest. In 1930, Gandhi campaigned to change the salt law. Under British law in India, all salt had to be bought from the government. A national protest began. Thousands of people were jailed. Many others were killed. However, the protest worked. In 1931, Britain changed the law.

Mahatma Gandhi

SALTY SAYING

To "take something with a pinch of salt" means to realize it may not be true. The saying may come from the idea that things are easier to swallow if they are flavored with a little salt.

1930

Indian women and children fill pots with salt water. They used the water to make their own salt. This was against the law in 1930.

19

HARVESTING SALT

All salt was once in water. When oceans dry up, they leave salt behind. Often the salt becomes part of rocks. Over time, the **minerals** in rocks and soil are dissolved by rain. They are carried back to the oceans by rivers and streams.

SEAWATER

The oldest way of getting salt is from seawater. It is called **solar** salt. In hot, dry climates, the sun causes the water to evaporate. The salt is left behind. Salt workers put the salt in piles.

Today, machines are sometimes used to harvest the salt. Seawater is pumped into a series of pans arranged in a **sequence**. The water evaporates gradually, leaving the minerals. Each of the minerals separates from the water at a different rate. Salt is almost the last mineral to separate. The **substance** in the final pan is likely to be about 98 percent sodium chloride, or salt.

Evaporation ponds
at Shark Bay, Australia

Each section on these pages has a heading and a photograph. That will help me understand the different ways that people get salt.

The hotel on the Uyuni salt flats
is completely built of salt.

SALT LAKES

Most lakes are freshwater. However, when a lake doesn't have any
rivers flowing out of it, the minerals in it build up. The lake becomes salty.

Sometimes lakes in deserts dry up in the heat, leaving the salt behind.
The largest salt flat in the world is the Salar de Uyuni in Bolivia.
About 40,000 years ago, it was part of a huge lake.

People use picks and shovels
to harvest salt from the salt flat.
They build small huts out
of blocks of salt. They live
in the huts while they work.

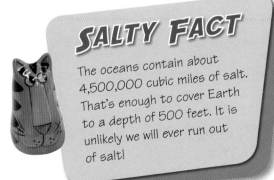

SALTY FACT

The oceans contain about
4,500,000 cubic miles of salt.
That's enough to cover Earth
to a depth of 500 feet. It is
unlikely we will ever run out
of salt!

Underground salt mine

ROCK SALT

Rock salt is found deep below the earth's surface. It was formed millions of years ago by the evaporation of oceans. To mine rock salt, workers dig tunnels down into the ground. They use drills to break off large blocks of the salt.

Rock salt

A common way of mining underground salt is the room and pillar method. The miners hollow out large "rooms" of salt. They leave pillars of salt that reach from the ground to the roof. The pillars support the ceiling of the mine so that it won't collapse. About half the salt is left in the mine.

SALT DOMES

Sometimes salt is
deep inside the earth.
Because salt is lighter
than most other minerals,
it can flow slowly upward,
like **magma**. It breaks through
the rock above it. It forms
a dome of salt. Salt domes can
be several miles across. They
can be up to six miles deep. They are
often surrounded by oil and natural gas.

SATELLITE PHOTOGRAPH

The rocks of
the Zagros Mountains
in Iran are forcing the
underground salt to rise
to the surface as
a salt dome.

Salt dome in Yemen

SALTY SAYING

A sailor is sometimes
called "an old salt."

23

SIMPLY ADD SALT

The taste buds on our tongues let us know what food tastes like. They can tell whether food is sweet, sour, salty, or bitter. People add salt to their food because salty food tastes good. Adding a dash of salt also enhances other flavors, such as sweet ones.

Salt helps to prevent **bacteria** and **mold** from growing on food. People cover food with salt to keep it from spoiling. They also soak food in brine to preserve it. This is called **pickling**. Many vegetables, fruits, and meats can be pickled. Pickled cabbage is called sauerkraut. Pickled pig's feet are a favorite food in parts of the United States and Ireland.

SALTY SAYING

To "salt something away" is to put it away to use in the future. The saying may come from the use of salt to preserve food.

Pickled cobra is a popular food in some countries.

When grass doesn't contain much sodium, farmers often give animals salt blocks to lick.

Salt has hundreds of uses. Most of them have nothing to do with food. When you use soap or toothpaste, you are using salt. Salt kills bacteria. It puts out grease fires. Salt softens water so that soap lathers more easily. It is used in the making of paper, plastics, glass, and **antifreeze**.

SALTY FACT

The words sauce, sausage, salami, and salad all come from the Latin word sal, meaning salt.

Half of the salt produced in America is spread on icy roads to help melt ice. Sometimes animals lick the road to get the salt their bodies need. Unfortunately, the salt run-off from the roads can kill trees.

BLOOD, SWEAT, AND TEARS

Blood, sweat, and tears contain salt. If you lick your skin when it is hot, you will probably taste salt. Lack of salt can make people sick and even kill them. Our cells cannot work properly without salt. People in hot places need more salt than people in cold places. That is because they sweat more.

Salt helps move our muscles, including the heart. The sodium and chloride in salt are **electrolytes**. They conduct electricity through the body, sending messages to the muscles.

Salt is important because:
- it helps food taste better
- it keeps food from spoiling
- it helps our muscles to move
- it helps conduct electricity in our bodies

Salt helps to move our muscles.

SALTY FACT

The salt in our bodies would fill three or four salt shakers.

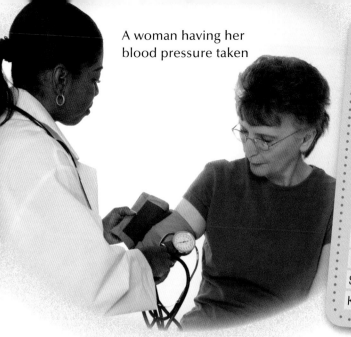

A woman having her blood pressure taken

Our brain keeps track of the amount of salt in our body. If there is too much, it comes out in our urine. Many doctors believe that too much salt can cause high blood pressure. High blood pressure is an increased pressure on the **arteries**. People may not realize they have high blood pressure. There are no obvious signs. It is called the silent killer.

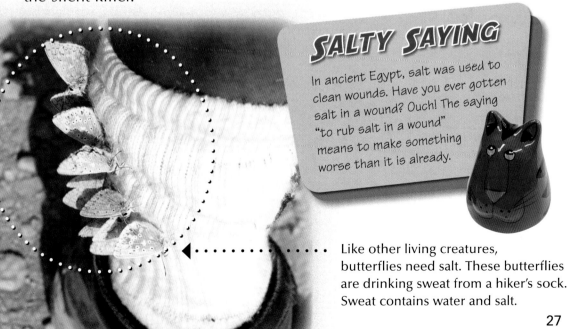

SALTY SAYING

In ancient Egypt, salt was used to clean wounds. Have you ever gotten salt in a wound? Ouch! The saying "to rub salt in a wound" means to make something worse than it is already.

Like other living creatures, butterflies need salt. These butterflies are drinking sweat from a hiker's sock. Sweat contains water and salt.

THE SALT TRADE

Salt used to be called "white gold." People traded salt for livestock, food, and clothing. They even traded it for slaves! Chinese emperors had their pictures stamped onto coins made of salt. The coins were used as money.

The salt trade has always been difficult and dangerous. In many countries, fuel is expensive and labor is still cheap. Therefore, the old ways of harvesting and transporting salt are still common.

Camels transport the salt across the Sahara desert in northwest Africa. They go from the salt mines at Taoudenni to the markets at Timbuktu. The camel caravans trudge 450 miles through sandstorms and blazing heat. There are no roads. It is important that traders find their way carefully. If they are wrong about where the next water hole is, they may die.

NORTHERN AFRICA

TAOUDENNI
ALGERIA
SAHARA
MAURITANIA
MALI
TIMBUKTU

A caravan of camels laden with salt crosses the Sahara.

Woman collecting salt in Mauritius

Salt seller in Timbuktu

From ancient times, salt was often traded in West Africa without any words being spoken. Sellers put piles of salt on the ground. Then they beat a drum and went away. Buyers came and put some gold beside the salt. Then they went away. The sellers came back. If there wasn't enough gold, they took away some of the salt. This went on until both parties agreed on the price.

Gold has been a symbol of wealth for as long as anyone can remember. So calling salt "white gold" meant it was very valuable. For the same reason, oil is sometimes called "black gold."

CHILD SALT WORKERS

The first sentence should help me figure out what the page is about. This page will probably be about how hard the work is. I often use the first sentence of a paragraph to help me figure out what to expect as I read.

Salt mining is very hard work. In places with few jobs, salt mining is often the only way for people to earn an income. In some parts of the world, children work in the salt mines alongside their parents. The children work for long hours in hot, **humid** conditions. Sometimes their work means they cannot go to school. If they do go to school, they usually leave before they finish elementary school.

Many salt workers do not wear protective clothing. The sun reflects off the white salt. The bright light can injure their eyes. Their hands and feet are damaged by the hard salt. They get sores that do not heal. They have health problems from breathing in salt.

Salt may not be as rare as early humans thought it was. However, it is still very precious to us. Even today, people risk their health and their lives to supply it to the world.

In some countries, there are no laws about working conditions. In some places, even children have to work long hours. They cannot go to school. If they do go, they are often too tired from working to learn.

Salt mines are often in places where the people are poor and there aren't many jobs.

Children working in a factory in Bangladesh

WHAT DO YOU THINK?

Is it okay to buy things made by children?

PRO

It's good to be able to buy things cheaply. Also, if we don't buy the things made by children, they will lose their jobs. Then their families will not have enough money. It would be better to write letters to try to get governments to make proper laws.

So are coffee and cocoa **plantations**. Often the whole family needs to work to earn enough money to live. When people are not paid much, the products they make can be sold cheaply.

Some people believe it is wrong to buy goods produced by child labor. They think it is **exploitation** of those children.

CON

If we buy things made by children, we are exploiting them too. That makes us as bad as the employers. If we do not buy these things, the employers might think about whether it's right to employ children. They might also start paying their adult workers a fair wage.

33

GLOSSARY

antifreeze a chemical substance that lowers the freezing point
of the substance around it

artery (*AR tuh ree*) a blood vessel that carries blood away from the heart

bacteria (*bak TIHR ee uh*) tiny living things that can cause disease
or kill pests

beer vinegar vinegar made from beer

blockade to block

civil war a war between two groups of people living in the same country

colony (*KOL uh nee*) a settlement under the rule of a parent country

exploit (*ek SPLOIT*) to take advantage of someone or something

humid (*HYOO mid*) having a large amount of water vapor in the air.
Humid air can feel damp and thick.

magma melted rock that is inside the earth

mold a fungus that grows on food and damp things

plantation (*plan TAY shuhn*) a large farm on which, usually,
only one crop is grown

revolution (*rev uh LOO shuhn*) an uprising by the people of
a country that changes the way in which the country is governed

sequence (*SEE kwenss*) an arrangement of things that follow
one after the other in a series

smuggle to bring something into a place illegally

terrace (*TER iss*) a flat field cut into the side of a hill or mountain

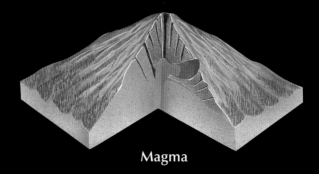

Magma

FIND OUT MORE

BOOKS

Bingham, Caroline. *Rocks and Minerals*. DK Publishing, 2004.

Blobaum, Cindy. *Geology Rocks!* Williamson Publishing Company, 1999.

Kurlansky, Mark. *The Story of Salt*. Putnam Juvenile, 2006.

Lilly, Melinda. *Salt*. Rourke Publishing, 2001.

Mecozzi, Maureen. *The Uncanny Can*. Scholastic Inc., 2008.

Ricciuti, Edward. *Rocks and Minerals*. Scholastic, 2001.

Zronik, John Paul. *Salt*. Crabtree Publishing Company, 2004.

WEB SITES

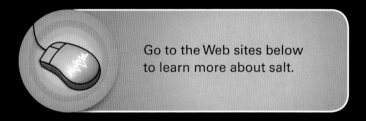

Go to the Web sites below to learn more about salt.

www.cargill.com/sf_bay/kidspage_harvest.htm

www.historyforkids.org/learn/food/salt.htm

www.rocksforkids.com

www.entertainment.howstuffworks.com/uses-for-salt-childrens-activities-ga.htm

INDEX

Africa   8, 28–29
American Civil War   17
American Revolution   17
animals   14–15, 24–25, 27–28
Bonneville, Utah   15
children   19, 31–33
China   9–10, 28
chloride   26
customs   13
Dead Sea   15
El Paso, Texas   18
food   8, 16–17, 24–28
French Revolution   16
Gandhi, Mahatma   19
Hallstatt, Austria   14
harvesting   20–23, 28, 33
human body   9, 15, 26–27
Maras, Peru   11

minerals   20–21, 23
place-names   14
rock salt   22
Rome   10, 16
Salar de Uyuni, Bolivia   21
salt domes   23
salt lakes   15, 21
salt mines   10–11, 14, 17, 22,
                          28, 31–32
salt wars   8, 16–19
sayings   10, 13, 19, 23–24, 27
seawater   15, 20–21
sodium   25–26
solar salt   20
Via Salaria, Rome   10
Wieliczka, Poland   10–11
workers   20–22, 28–33

ABOUT THE AUTHOR

Laura Layton Strom is the author of many fiction and nonfiction books for children. She has worked as an educational writer, editor, and publisher for more than 20 years. Laura is fascinated with how important common salt has been in our history. She hopes young people learn some surprising salt facts that they can use to dazzle their family and friends!